HOW TO DRAW BIG CATS

Grrrr!

Carolyn Franklin

BOOK HOUSE

Published in Great Britain in 2006 by
Book House, an imprint of
The Salariya Book Company Ltd
25 Marlborough Place, Brighton, BN1 1UB

3 5 7 9 8 6 4 2

SALARIYA

Please visit The Salariya Book Company at: **www.salariya.com**

Author: Carolyn Franklin is a graduate of Brighton College of
Art, England, specialising in design and illustration. She has
worked in animation, advertising and children's fiction and
non-fiction. She has a particular interest in natural history and
has written and illustrated many books on the subject.

Editors: Sophie Izod, Karen Smith
Editorial Assistant: Mark Williams

PB ISBN-10: 1-904642-68-3
PB ISBN-13: 978-1-904642-68-8

A CIP catalogue record for this book is available
from the British Library.

Printed and bound in China.
Printed on paper from sustainable sources.
Reprinted in 2009.

*Fixatives should be used under
adult supervision.

Contents

Making a start

Drawing is great fun and very exciting! You don't need expensive equipment. Use whatever materials are handy: scraps of paper, cardboard packaging or old greeting cards. Try using pencils, crayons, marker-pens or charcoal. You can draw with paint too, using a brush, a stick or even your finger.

Grrrr!

Soft pencil

Start by doodling and experimenting with shapes and patterns.

Finger print and black felt-tip pen

Pencil shading

Felt-tip dots

Finger print and felt-tip

Black felt–tip pen with
clear water wash and
hard pencil

Textures

Wet a sheet of paper and draw on it with a
felt–tip pen. See how the ink runs and the
lines soften. Experiment by drawing on papers
with different textures. Try sketching in white
pastel on black or grey paper (see page 6).

Sketching

Carry a sketch pad with you at all
times. Your drawing will get better the
more you draw and sketch.

A sketch pad is your working
record of ideas and
ways of drawing.

Ball–point pen and
hard pencil

Ball–point pen

Grey felt–tip pen with clear
water wash and hard pencil

Grey felt–tip pen and pencil shading

Pencil finger print and ink wash

5

Drawing tools

Here are just a few of the many tools that you can use for drawing. Let your imagination go and have fun experimenting with all the different marks you can make.

Pencil

Watercolour pencil

Charcoal pencil

Charcoal stick

Pastels

Finger painting

Black, grey and white pastel on grey sugar paper

Each grade of **pencil** makes a different mark, from fine, grey lines through to soft, black ones. Hard pencils are graded as H, 2H, 3H, 4H, 5H and 6H (the hardest). An HB pencil is ideal for general sketching. Soft pencils are graded from B, 2B, 3B, 4B, 5B to 6B (the softest and blackest).

Watercolour pencils come in many different colours and make a line similar to an HB pencil. Paint over your finished drawing with clean water and the lines will soften and run.

It is less messy and easier to achieve a fine line with a **charcoal pencil** than a **charcoal stick**. Create soft tones by smudging lines with your finger. Spray with fixative* to prevent further smudging (see page 2).

Pastels are brittle sticks of powdered colour. They blend and smudge easily and are ideal for quick sketches. Pastel drawings work well on textured, coloured paper. Spray your drawing with fixative* when your drawing is finished (see page 2).

Experiment with finger painting. Your finger prints make exciting patterns and textures. Use your fingers to smudge soft pencil, charcoal and pastel lines.

Ball-point pens are very useful for sketching and making notes. Make different tones by building up layers of shading.

A **mapping pen** has to be dipped into bottled ink to fill the nib. Different nib shapes make different marks. Try putting a diluted ink wash over parts of the finished drawing.

Draftsman's pens and specialist art pens can produce extremely fine lines and are ideal for creating fur markings. A variety of pen nibs are available which produce different widths of line.

Felt-tip pens are ideal for quick sketches. If the ink is not waterproof, try drawing on wet paper and see the effect.

Broad nibbed marker pens make interesting lines and are good for large, bold sketches. Try using a black pen for the main sketch and a grey one to block in areas of shadow.

Paintbrushes are shaped differently to make different marks. Japanese brushes are soft and produce beautiful flowing lines. Large sable brushes are good for painting a wash over a line drawing. Fine brushes are good for drawing the delicate lines of whiskers and fur.

Ball-point pen

Mapping pen

Draftsman's pen

Felt-tip pen

Marker pen

Paintbrush

7

Anatomy

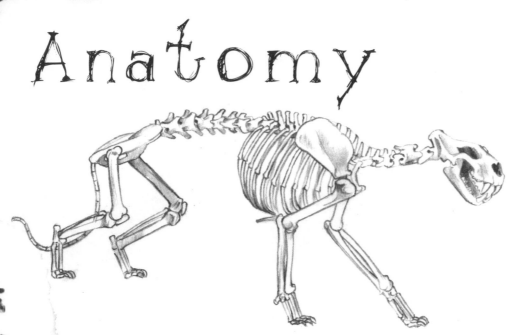

Skeleton of a leopard

Musculature of a leopard

Study the skeleton. See how the leopard's front and back legs bend. Look at the position of the muscles and see how they wrap around the skeleton.

Movement and muscles

Watch the movement of a domestic cat to see how it walks, runs and lies down. Compare the drawing of the leopard's skeleton to the drawing on this page. Understanding how an animal's skeleton moves and where its major muscles lie, will help to make your drawings more realistic and lively.

Look and learn

Some cats have a longer, leaner look than others. Study each cat before you start to draw.

See how this leopard's back curves

Using photographs

It is always best to draw something you can actually see. However, you can still produce a lifelike drawing by using a photograph as reference.

Drawing from photographs

Grids

Make a tracing of the photograph and draw a grid over it (above).

Tracing

Lightly draw another grid in the same proportions on your drawing paper. You can now transfer the shapes from your tracing to your drawing paper using these grids as a guide (left). This method is called **squaring up**.

Light source

Drawing in three dimensions

A drawing of a photograph can look too flat.
Make your drawing look more three-dimensional
by checking how light falls on the tiger's head
and then shade in the dark areas.

Areas of shade

Tones and focal points

Draw in the mid-tone grey fur. Leave areas
of the paper untouched for white fur. Pay
special attention when drawing the cat's eyes
as they are the focal point of the drawing.
Draw in the dark stripes and finally use a
fine paint brush with white paint to draw
the whiskers.

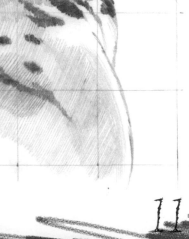

Style and medium

You can transform a drawing simply by changing the medium you use.

Try drawing the same image but using different techniques and on various types and sizes of paper.

This tiger cub was sketched in charcoal with a light wash of black watercolour.

This snow leopard was drawn with a felt-tip pen. Then a light wash of water was painted over parts of it.

Black and white pastels were used on grey textured paper to draw this leopard.

This tiger was first drawn in pencil. Masking fluid was painted over some areas of the picture and then a watercolour wash was added. When dry the masking fluid was rubbed off using a soft eraser. These areas have been kept white.

13

Tiger

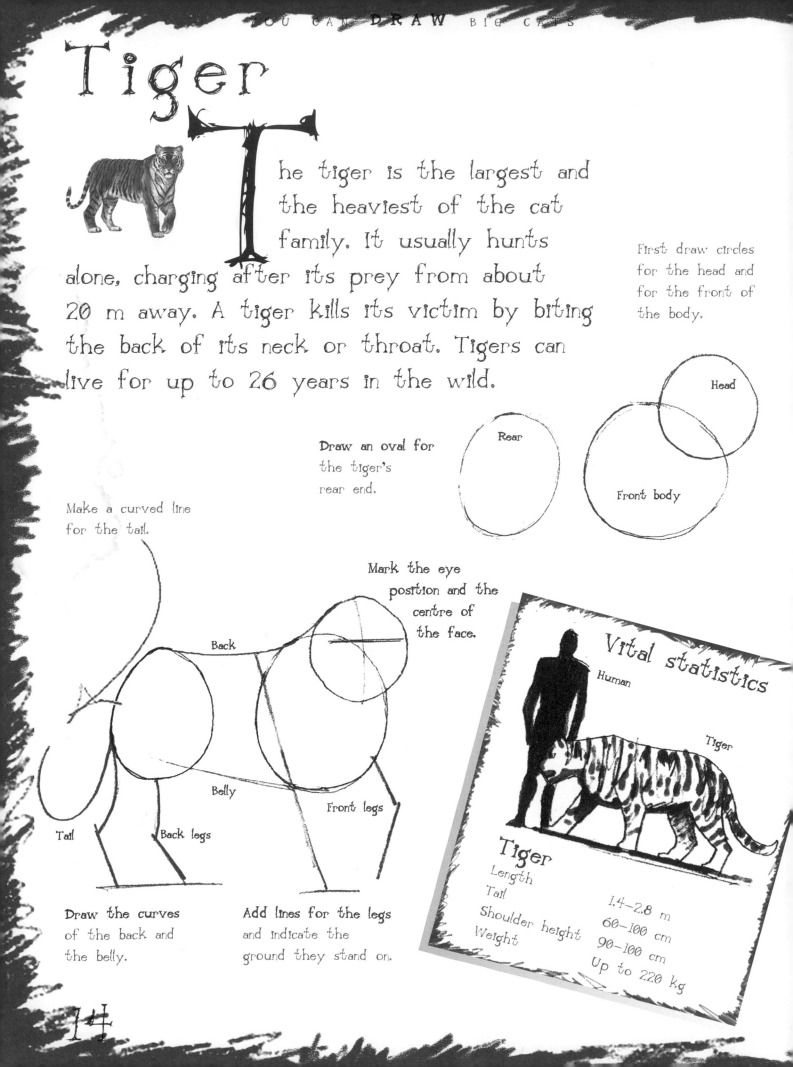

The tiger is the largest and the heaviest of the cat family. It usually hunts alone, charging after its prey from about 20 m away. A tiger kills its victim by biting the back of its neck or throat. Tigers can live for up to 26 years in the wild.

First draw circles for the head and for the front of the body.

Head

Front body

Draw an oval for the tiger's rear end.

Rear

Make a curved line for the tail.

Mark the eye position and the centre of the face.

Back

Belly

Tail

Back legs

Front legs

Draw the curves of the back and the belly.

Add lines for the legs and indicate the ground they stand on.

Vital statistics

Human

Tiger

Tiger

Length	1.4–2.8 m
Tail	60–100 cm
Shoulder height	90–100 cm
Weight	Up to 220 kg

Draw in the ears.

Draw lines for the eyes
and for the position
of the nose and mouth.

Finish the shape
of the tail.

Nose

Mouth

When drawing the legs
and feet, imagine the
tiger's body is a tube
with legs set into it.

Draw the tiger's
face and stripes.

Draw the stripes with
a soft black pencil
using marks that
follow the fur's
direction.

A tiger's orange and black stripes
provide it with subtle camouflage
in dappled light and shade.

15

Lion

The magnificent lion is the second largest of the big cats. Fully grown males can weigh over 230 kg and can measure over 3 m long from tail tip to nose. A lion's roar can be heard up to 8 km away and is the loudest sound made by any big cat.

Draw circles for the head, muzzle and rear and a large oval for the front of the body.

Head

Rear

Muzzle

Belly

Front

Draw lines under the belly and up to the muzzle.

Proportion

Use the size of the lion's head as a unit of measurement to help keep your drawing in proportion. The lion is 3 heads tall and its body is 3.5 heads long.

Mark out the eye line and the sides of the muzzle.

Back

Mane

Add lines for the position of the legs and the lion's feet. Draw lines for the back and tail.

Tail

Legs

Sketch in circles for the lion's mane and ears.

Draw a curved line to show the high arch of a lion's back.

Lightly draw in the shape of the eyes, nose and mouth.

Extend the line of the mane down to its belly.

Sketch in the front of the legs and the lion's paws.

Make the lion's hindquarters more angular.

Draw the lion's mane using your pencil marks to follow the direction of the hair.

Finish drawing in the eyes, the nose and the mouth.

Finish drawing the hindquarters. Shade in the muscles.

A lion's mane can make a lion appear to be larger in size, which scares away other male lions.

17

Panther

A panther is a leopard or a jaguar with a black coat. Panthers are found in dense, dark tropical rainforests where their colouring camouflages them well for hunting.

Chiaroscuro — Light and shade
When drawing a dark object, look to see which direction the light is coming from. Draw in the darkest parts of your subject first. Slowly build up the grey areas leaving some white paper showing through as the lightest parts of your drawing.

Draw circles for the head, front and rear of the body.

Back

Head

Rear

Belly

Front

Put in lines for the back and belly.

Tail

Indicate the panther's eye position and draw a circle for its muzzle.

Sketch in a long curved tail.

Neck

Eyes

Muzzle

Back legs

Draw in curved and straight lines for the back legs and feet.

Add lines for its neck, front legs and feet.

Front legs

18

Finish drawing the tail. Sketch in the curve of the back and belly.

Add the back and front of the neck.

Draw in the ears, nose and mouth.

Ears

Back legs

Belly

Front legs

Paws

Draw the front of the legs and the shape of the paws.

Round off any sharp corners. Shade in the light and dark areas of fur (as explained opposite).

Finish drawing the panther's face and ears.

Stand the panther firmly on the ground so he is not floating!

Panthers often attack from behind, dragging their prey up into trees to eat later.

19

Tiger's head

An average male tiger stands 90 cm tall at shoulder height. Unlike other members of the cat family, tigers are not good tree climbers. However, they are strong swimmers and in floods they are known to swim in search of stranded prey.

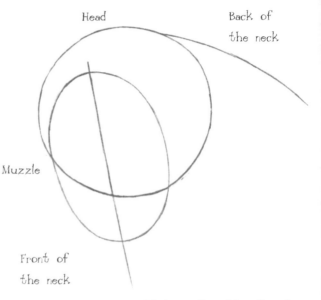

Draw a circle for the head and an oval for the muzzle.

Head

Back of the neck

Muzzle

Front of the neck

Add lines for the front and back of the neck.

Eyes

Highlight

Shadow

Eyes are often the focal point of a drawing. Study and sketch the eyes of different animals. Look at the highlight on the eye and at the shape of the pupil.

Look carefully at the angle of the ears and draw them in. Indicate the eye position.

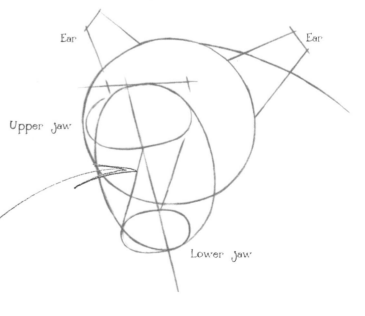

Ear

Ear

Upper jaw

Lower jaw

Draw two ovals, one for the lower jaw and the other for the upper jaw.

Draw two lines to join the lower jaw to the back of the mouth.

The maximum lifespan of a tiger is usually around 26 years and for most of their lives, tigers live alone.

Draw in the fur on either side of its face.

Draw in the large front teeth (top and bottom).

Draw the tiger's gums and the position of its back teeth.

Draw the screwed-up face and eyes of the tiger.

Sketch in the shape of the tiger's stripes. Block in the areas of grey tone first, and then the areas of dark tone.

Lastly, use a fine paint brush and white paint for the paler whiskers.

Leopard

eopards are agile climbers and often haul their prey into the branches of a tree. They hunt alone and mainly at night. Each leopard has its own territory that it defends from other leopards.

Draw circles for the leopard's rear end, head and muzzle.

Rear

Head

Front leg

Muzzle

Sketch in the curve of the neck and back and the line of the front leg.

Draw the long curved line of the tail.

Tail

Back leg

Paw

Add straight lines for the back leg, and draw circles for the paws.

Draw a circle for one ear, and a triangle for the other.

Ears

Mark the position of the eyes and the muzzle.

Paw

Make the leg shapes rounded to show the muscles in the legs and finish the paws.

Sketch in the neckline and the side of the face. Lightly draw in the eyes and nose. Add the lower jaw.

A leopard's spots make perfect camouflage in the dappled shade of a forest.

Lightly sketch in the leopard's markings.

Draw in the detail of the eyes, nose, ears and mouth.

Sketch in a tree branch. Look at the direction of light and put shadows under the leopard.

Finally, use white paint and a fine paintbrush to add the leopard's whiskers.

Lynx

ynx are smaller than many other big cats. They live alone, mainly in pine forests, high up on mountain slopes. A lynx has a stubby tail, long tufted ears, a short body and large feet.

Draw circles for the head, front and rear ends of the lynx.

Front

Head

Rear

Construction lines

Study these drawings of a polar bear and a brown bear. Compare ear and shapes. Check the position of their features. Using construction lines helps create three-dimensional looking drawings.

Sketch in the curve of the back and tail.

Back

Tail

Lightly mark a cross at the centre of the head.

Put in straight lines for the back legs.

Back legs

Draw lines for the front legs and add circles for the paws.

Front legs

Paws

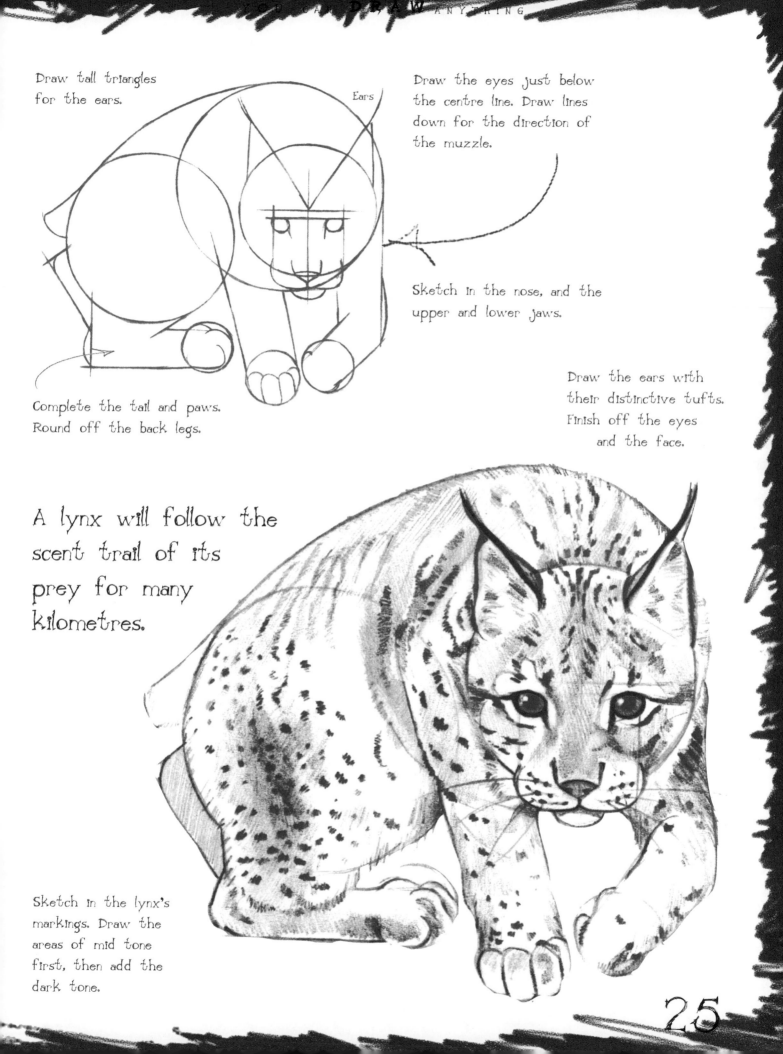

Draw tall triangles
for the ears.

Ears

Draw the eyes just below
the centre line. Draw lines
down for the direction of
the muzzle.

Sketch in the nose, and the
upper and lower jaws.

Complete the tail and paws.
Round off the back legs.

Draw the ears with
their distinctive tufts.
Finish off the eyes
and the face.

A lynx will follow the
scent trail of its
prey for many
kilometres.

Sketch in the lynx's
markings. Draw the
areas of mid tone
first, then add the
dark tone.

25

Cheetah

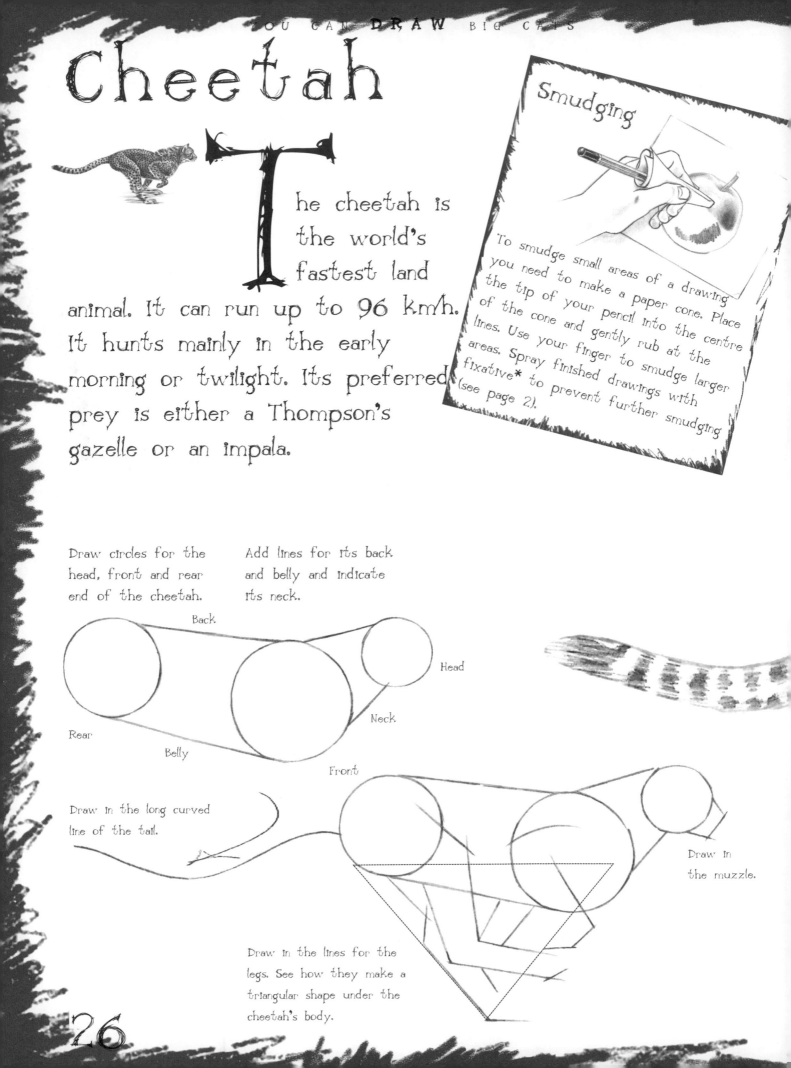

The cheetah is the world's fastest land animal. It can run up to 96 km/h. It hunts mainly in the early morning or twilight. Its preferred prey is either a Thompson's gazelle or an impala.

Smudging

To smudge small areas of a drawing you need to make a paper cone. Place the tip of your pencil into the centre of the cone and gently rub at the lines. Use your finger to smudge larger areas. Spray finished drawings with fixative* to prevent further smudging (see page 2).

Draw circles for the head, front and rear end of the cheetah.

Add lines for its back and belly and indicate its neck.

Back

Head

Neck

Rear

Belly

Front

Draw in the long curved line of the tail.

Draw in the muzzle.

Draw in the lines for the legs. See how they make a triangular shape under the cheetah's body.

26

Finish the tail. It acts as a counterbalance to the rest of the cheetah's body.

Draw the ears and mane.

Curve the lines of the cheetah's back and belly.

Sketch in the eye, nose and mouth.

A cheetah has a streamlined body and a small head. Its long legs and flexible spine give the cheetah the maximum length of stride necessary for great speed.

Finish the legs and sketch in the paws. Round off all sharp angles.

Draw the cheetah's spotted coat. The tail markings begin as spots but gradually become stripes.

Draw in the face markings.

To give the impression of speed, carefully smudge both hind legs. (The drawing should still show through).

27

Lion cubs

Lions live in family groups called prides. Each pride consists of several females, their cubs and at least one male. Lion cubs start learning to hunt at about 11 months old but cannot catch prey until they are nearly 16 months old. A cub weighs about 1.3 kg at birth and up to 230 kg when adult.

Draw a circle for the head of the top cub and a line for its neck. Mark in its eye level.

Head

Neck

Head

Draw two circles for the head and body of the lower cub. Mark in its eye level.

Body of right cub

Ear

Draw circles for the ears and muzzles of both cubs.

Mark the position of their eyes.

Muzzle

Ear

Muzzle

Front legs

Draw in lines for their front legs and ovals for paws.

Composition

An important part of creating a good drawing is your composition. Use a small cardboard frame of the same proportion as your drawing paper, to help you judge your composition. Hold the frame in front of your subject and more it around to try different views.

Study each cub's expression before drawing their eyes. Draw in each cub's nose and mouth.

Put dark tones on the faces.

Sketch in the ears. Finish drawing the paws and the front legs. Draw in the top cub's neck.

Puma

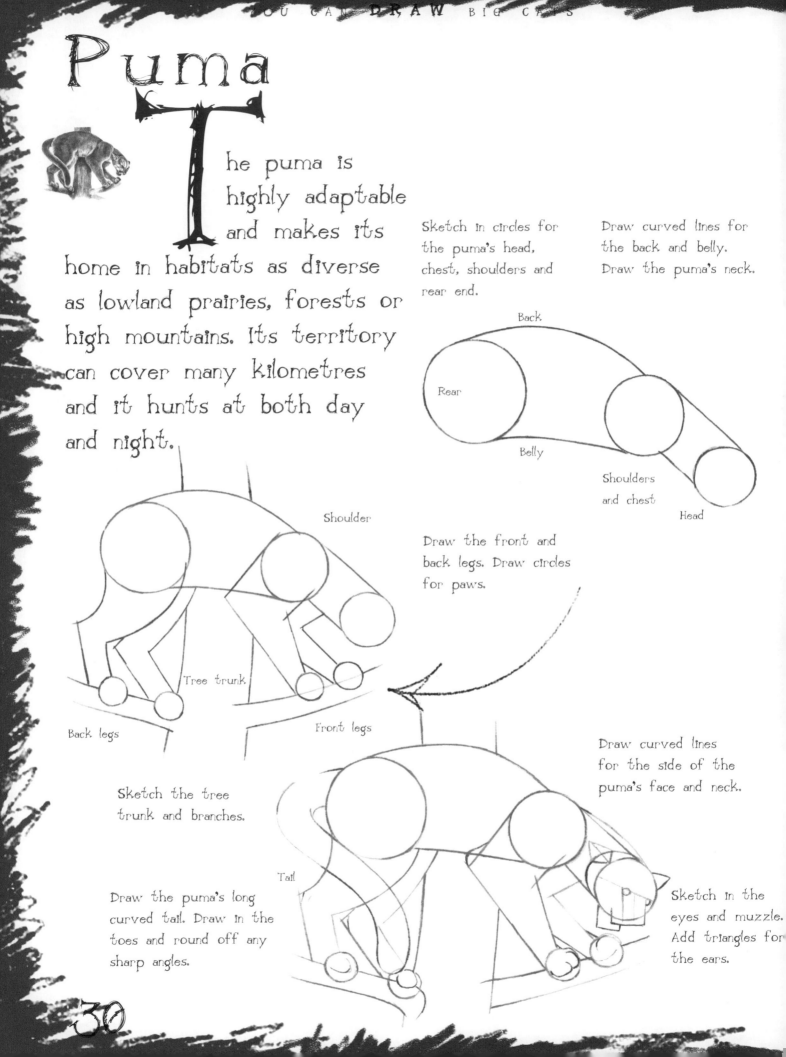

The puma is highly adaptable and makes its home in habitats as diverse as lowland prairies, forests or high mountains. Its territory can cover many kilometres and it hunts at both day and night.

Sketch in circles for the puma's head, chest, shoulders and rear end.

Draw curved lines for the back and belly. Draw the puma's neck.

Back

Rear

Belly

Shoulders and chest

Head

Shoulder

Draw the front and back legs. Draw circles for paws.

Tree trunk

Back legs

Front legs

Sketch the tree trunk and branches.

Draw curved lines for the side of the puma's face and neck.

Tail

Draw the puma's long curved tail. Draw in the toes and round off any sharp angles.

Sketch in the eyes and muzzle. Add triangles for the ears.

A puma is a skillful
jumper. From standing
it can leap onto a
branch several metres
off the ground.

Checking your drawing

When you finish your initial sketch
hold it up to a mirror to check. The
image will be in reverse and it will
make any mistakes stand out.

Draw the puma's fur
(notice that the fur on
the tail is darker).

Block in the shadow
cast on the tree by
the puma.

Draw in the eyes, eye
markings and ears.

31

Glossary

Chiaroscuro The use of light and dark shades in a drawing or painting.

Composition The position of a picture on the drawing paper.

Construction lines Structural lines used in the early stages of a drawing.

Fixative A type of resin used to spray over a finished drawing to prevent smudging* (see page 2).

Focal point A central point of interest.

Light source The direction the light is coming from.

Masking fluid A thin rubber solution, applied by brush to block off an area of a painting. It is peeled or rubbed off when dry.

Proportion The correct relationship of scale between parts of a drawing.

Reference Photographs or other images that can be drawn, if drawing from life is not possible.

Squaring up To transfer a drawing or photo accurately using square grids.

Three-dimensional An image that has the effect of making it look lifelike or real.

Index